MW01134935

KINGFISHER
LONDON & NEW YORK

KINGFISHER
LONDON & NEW YORK

Text and illustration copyright © Macmillan Publishers International Ltd 2025
First published in 2025 in the United States by Kingfisher
120 Broadway, New York, NY 10271
Kingfisher is an imprint of
Macmillan Children's Books, London

Distributed in the U.S. and Canada by Macmillan,
120 Broadway, New York, NY 10271

Library of Congress Cataloging-in-Publication Data has been applied for

ISBN 978-0-7534-8121-9

This book is not authorized, licensed, or endorsed by Harry Styles or any affiliate.

Kingfisher books are available for special promotions and premiums.
For details contact: Special Markets Department, Macmillan,
120 Broadway, New York, NY 10271

For more information, please visit
www.kingfisherbooks.com

Printed in China
2 4 6 8 9 7 5 3 1

EU representative: 1st Floor, The Liffey Trust Centre,
117-126 Sheriff Street Upper, Dublin 1 D01 YC43

FSC
www.fsc.org

MIX
Paper | Supporting
responsible forestry
FSC® C116313

Let's Meet
HARRY

ILLUSTRATED BY MARIANA AVILA LAGUNES
WRITTEN BY CLAIRE BAKER

When Harry was born in 1994, he lived in a small town in the middle of England with his mom Anne, dad Desmond, and big sister Gemma.

When he was seven, the family moved north to a pretty village called Holmes Chapel.

Harry's grandfather bought him a
karaoke machine. They had a lot of fun
singing along to his favorite songs.

5

By the time he was 15,
Harry was the lead singer in a
band with three of his school friends.

MEMORIES

A.M.

The friends decided to enter a music competition at their school.

#1

They were very excited when they came in first!

When he wasn't at school or singing in the band, Harry worked at a local bakery. The customers would often hear him singing!

But Harry knew he wouldn't work in the bakery forever.

When he was 16, his mom saw a chance for
Harry to become a professional singer.
They traveled to the city of Manchester, England.

Harry auditioned for *The X Factor*, a popular television talent show. The judges didn't like the first song he sang, so he tried a different one.

It worked! He was through to the next round, but that was where his dream nearly ended. Harry was about to head home.

But the judges saw he had star quality and had another plan for him . . .

They asked him to stay and form a new pop group with four other singers.

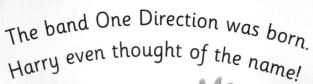

The band One Direction was born.
Harry even thought of the name!

Harry, Liam, Louis, Niall, and Zayn
loved singing together. They performed
in the competition every week and
made it to the big *X Factor* final.

Although the band didn't come in first, Harry's dream of being a singer wasn't over yet.

ONE DIRECTION

After the show finished, One Direction signed a recording contract, and Harry's life as a pop star really began.

Less than a year later, One Direction's first single, "What Makes You Beautiful," raced up the charts.

Soon their first album came out. It was called *Up All Night*.

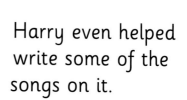

Harry even helped write some of the songs on it.

One Direction already had a lot of fans.
They were called Directioners.

Harry and his bandmates began their first world tour. Huge crowds watched every show and loved singing along to all of the songs.

One Direction had number one hits all over the world.
At just 17 years old, Harry was a star.

One Direction became one of the most popular boy bands ever. They made four more hit albums and toured around the world another three times.

They won lots of awards and even made a movie!

After six years together, One Direction decided it was time to take a break. Their fans were sad, but everyone was excited to see what Harry would do next.

Harry decided to go solo.
His songs were hits everywhere,
and he soon began his first world tour.

He enjoyed wearing exciting outfits
made by his favorite fashion designers.

Everyone loved to see what
bold and colorful outfits
Harry would wear!

21

Now Harry's fans had a new name, the Harries. Harry doesn't like any of them to ever feel left out. He reminds them how important it is to be who you want to be and to always be kind to each other. He even wrote a song about kindness.

Harry loves it when his fans dress up to watch his shows. A lot of them become as glamorous and sparkly as Harry himself.

Harry ended a world tour with fifteen shows at a huge concert arena called Madison Square Garden in New York.

He asked his fans to wear costumes for the show on Halloween. Harry dressed up too and renamed the night "Harryween"!

HARRY STYLES 15

On the last night he performed there,
Harry watched a special banner
appear, to celebrate all fifteen shows.

But Harry isn't just a singer—he's starred in movies too. From playing a soldier and a policeman to acting in a superhero movie, he always enjoys trying something new.

Harry's also a model, and he loves fashion. He often tries out unique outfits and isn't afraid to wear exactly what he likes.

When Harry isn't singing, acting, or modeling,
he's often busy collecting awards all over
the world. He's won over 100 for his music!

29

Despite all his success, Harry never forgets that some people aren't as lucky as he is, and he helps them out whenever he can.

He once cut off his hair and donated it to charity.